People Who Have Helped the World

MARIE CURIE

by Beverley Birch

Picture Credits

Bridgeman Art Library — 20-21, 24; British Nuclear Fuels — 6, 34 (all), 61; Central Electricity Generating Board — 60; E.T. Archive — 11; Exley Picture Library: Stefan Baluk — 4, 5, 7 (below), 8 (both), 9, 13, 14, 16 (top), 19, 23, 25, 27, 31, 36 (both), 40, 42 (both), 44, 49, 51, 54 (both): Wojciech Broniarek 7 (top), 38, 39, 56, (both) 57, (all); GeoScience Features Picture Library — 35; Imperial War Museum — 55; National Radiation Board — 47 (both); Ann Ronan Picture Library — 29 (both); Solvay et Cie, Brussels — 58.
Map drawn by Geoffrey Pleasance; paintings on cover and pages 33 and 53 by Borin Van Loon.

The Publishers thank William Heinemann Ltd. of London for their kind pemission to quote extracts from *Madame Curie*, Eve Curie's biography of her mother, and William Collins, Sons and Co. Ltd. of London for their kind permission to quote extracts from Robert Reid's biography, *Marie Curie*.

North American edition first published in 1988 by
Gareth Stevens, Inc.
7317 W. Green Tree Road
Milwaukee, WI 53223 USA

First published in the United Kingdom in 1988 with an
original text © 1988 by Exley Publications Ltd.
Additional end matter © 1988 by Gareth Stevens, Inc.

Library of Congress Cataloging-in-Publication Data

Birch, Beverley
    Marie Curie
    (People who have helped the world)
    "First published in the United Kingdom in 1988 with an original text © by
Exley Publications Ltd. and Gareth Stevens, Inc." — Verso t.p.
    Includes index.
    Summary: A biography of the chemist whose work with radium laid the
foundation for much of today's scientific knowledge.
    1. Curie, Marie, 1867-1934 — Juvenile literature. 2. Chemists — Poland
— Biography — Juvenile literature. 3. Statesmen — India — Biography —
Juvenile literature. [1. Curie, Marie, 1867-1934. 2. Chemists] I. Title.
QD22.C8B57 1988   530'.092'4 [B] [92]   88-2091
ISBN 1-55532-843-1
ISBN 1-55532-818-0 (lib. bdg.)

Series conceived and edited by Helen Exley.
Picture research: Diana Briscoe.
Research assistant: Margaret Montgomery.
Series editor, U.S.: Rhoda Irene Sherwood.
Editorial assistant, U.S.: Mary Thomas
Additional end matter, U.S.: Ric Hawthorne.

Printed in Hungary

1 2 3 4 5 6 7 8 9 93 92 91 90 89 88

MARIE CURIE

The Polish scientist who discovered radium and its life-saving properties

by Beverley Birch

Gareth Stevens Publishing
Milwaukee

The radiant glow

It was a cold winter's night in Paris, in the year 1902. In the icy damp of a ramshackle shed, two people stood side by side in the dark. Around them dozens of glowworms hovered, glimmering with a mysteriously beautiful light, and their glow held the promise of unimagined knowledge.

To the two watchers this was the pinnacle of their lives, a rare moment of absolute peace; for the two were Marie and Pierre Curie, the brilliant young scientists whose recent discovery of radium had taken the world by storm.

At the beginning, when they first suspected they had found something unbelievably powerful, something quite unknown, hidden in the rock they were examining, Pierre told Marie that he hoped it would be beautiful.

And here it was, in the tiny glass containers of precious radium – these glimmering liquids and crystals. Placed on the makeshift tables and shelves of the Curies' shed-laboratory, they seemed suspended in the darkness. Only the luminous blue glow indicated their presence.

Each was the product of months of painstaking, exhausting work. The story of their effort was etched deep in the lines of tiredness on the young couple's faces. Years later, Marie would write of how, as they looked around them at this shed which had become the focus of their lives, the soft glow of their radium filled her with "new emotion and delight."

And so they stood, unspeaking, linked in their silence by pride at their shared achievement and by the understanding that they had truly opened a vast new field of knowledge to the world – the science of radioactivity.

Opposite and below: Marie and Pierre Curie working in an old shed in Paris. This dilapidated, under-equipped shed was Marie's only laboratory and it was here that she worked for over four years and discovered radium. Her research also led scientists to the understanding of the atom. Marie could have become a millionaire, but she gave up all the financial rewards that followed the discoveries. She also gave her time, her family life, and, ultimately, her health.

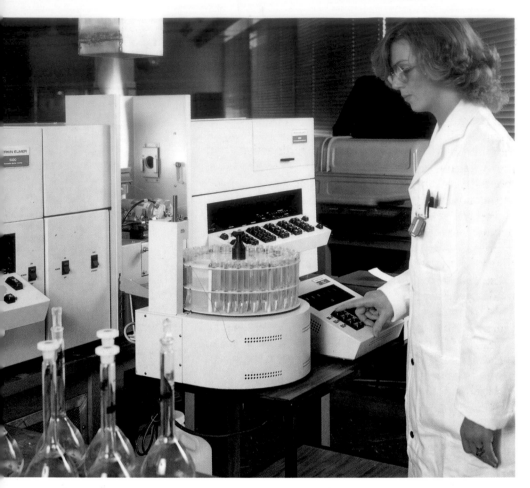

The new radioactivity

Nowadays radioactivity is an important part of everyday life. Scientists know what it is, how to use it, and how to make it. Nuclear power stations and submarines run on its energy. With it, industries as varied as paper-making and metal-rolling control the quality of their products. In the improvement of crops and livestock, the tracing of pollution in rivers, the testing of steel and concrete structures beneath the oceans, radioactivity plays a vital role. And in hospitals, it is used to sterilize equipment and to diagnose and treat disease – not least, cancer.

At the turn of the century, scientists knew only that a metal called uranium gave off some strange

Marie Curie would have been pleased to see women scientists now working alongside men and accepted on an equal footing. She would also have been amazed at how much money is now poured into scientific research, compared with the spartan conditions for scientists in her day.

and very powerful invisible rays. But what were they? Why did it happen? It was a mystery.

It caught the attention and the curiosity of young Marie Curie. She decided to explore it. Metals, rocks, sands, all the different materials she could lay her hands on – which would give off these rays? She set off on her determined course into unknown territory. In doing this, she discovered radium – more than a million times more radioactive than the uranium scientists already knew about. Here indeed was something powerful enough to unlock the secrets of the rays!

But the exploration of radioactivity did more. It began to reveal the answers to science's most fundamental mystery. Scientists began to understand the tiniest and most basic building block in the world – the one from which everything in the world is made – the atom.

Marie's work on radium is one of the central pillars on which the science of the modern world is founded. The story of radium's discovery is the story of Marie herself: a small, shy person, quiet, but strong and sure, and very, very determined.

Her story begins not in France but in the city of Warsaw, in the country of her birth, Poland.

Childhood in Poland

In one of the cobbled streets of Warsaw, near the battlements of the old city walls and not far from the swirling waters of the River Vistula, there is a house with a simple plaque beside the door. Proudly it announces that here, on November 7, 1867, Marie Curie was born – except that her name then was Marya Sklodowska, though she was known to her family as Manya. Three sisters – Sofia, aged six; Bronya, aged three; and Hela, a baby of eighteen months – awaited her birth with noisy impatience. On the other hand, four-year-old Joseph took his role as the only young man seriously, amid the noisy bustle of the girls' boarding school where the family lived in a few small rooms on the second floor. Their mother was principal there, and even during the first few days of Marie's life, she and their father

Above: 16 Freta Street, Warsaw in Poland where Marya Sklodowska, later Marie Curie, was born. The building was a small boarding school for girls and Marie's mother was the school principal.

On the wall of 16 Freta Street, which is now a museum dedicated to Marie Sklodowska-Curie, is this plaque that commemorates her birth on November 7, 1867.

7

Above: Wladislaw Sklodowski, Marie's father, was professor of physics and mathematics at a high school in Warsaw. He spoke many languages and read to his children regularly. He gave them all a love of literature and knowledge.

Marie's mother was seriously ill with TB when this photo was taken. She died when Marie was ten. An accomplished musician, she ran a private school in Warsaw.

struggled to cope with the incessant demands of school and pupils.

This was always the kind of atmosphere in which the family lived: shrill voices filling the air with chatter and shrieks; the sing-song of children struggling with their reading; impatient young feet pounding up and down the staircases and clattering on the floorboards above them.

It was nevertheless a close, loving and happy family, and during these years Marie forged bonds of friendship and understanding with her brother and sisters which lasted all her life. We know quite a lot about her from the letters she wrote to them over the years.

Marie's early life was also a time when the love of learning was instilled deep in the growing child. To have culture and knowledge, to use your mind and thoughts to become useful in the world, to enrich your experience more and more and more, these were the aims which their teacher-parents held high before them. They took deep root in all the children. Marie's father, in particular, was an unusual man. He was a quiet, soft-spoken person, with a precise mind and immense knowledge. He spoke not only Polish and Russian, but also French, German, Greek and Latin. He translated the literature of these languages into Polish so that his children could enjoy it, too.

Marie had one very strong memory. She stood in front of a polished glass case in her father's study, rising on tiptoe to see inside. What a collection of tubes and bottles, delicate and shining glass! Tiny dishes and scales, minute pieces of rock, a mysterious machine – what were they?

"Physics apparatus," her father told her. Little did the four-year-old Marie realize that in time these would be the tools of her own brilliant work.

By the age of five, Marie could read fluently. She read everything and anything she could lay her hands on: stories, poetry, history. As she grew a little older, even though she couldn't really understand most of it, she even buried herself in textbooks and technical papers borrowed from her father's library.

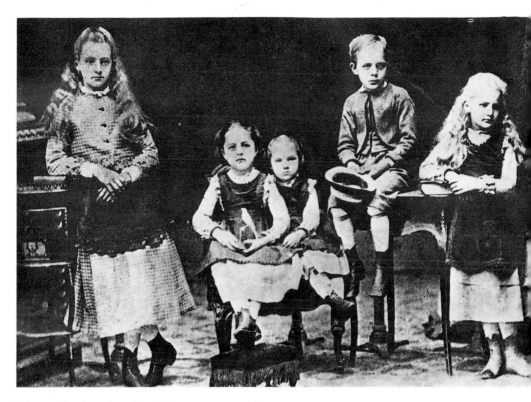

Tragedy in the family

Yet a cloud loomed darkly over the young family. Their mother grew sick. Since Marie's birth she had suffered from tuberculosis, a serious and infectious disease of the lungs. As Marie reached the age of six, her mother's illness grew worse. Their father scraped together enough money to send her for a year's rest and treatment at an expensive sanatorium in France.

This only raised false hopes. When she returned she looked older and exhausted. She was no better. The children began to fear the quickly-hidden, bloodstained handkerchiefs into which she coughed with a dry, painful sound.

Then some of the school pupils fell ill. Typhus, the doctors said. Bronya and Sofia caught the fever, and for weeks their bodies burned with it. Slowly Bronya grew better. Sofia never recovered. On a cold Wednesday in January of 1876, they saw her

Marie's brother and sisters, from left to right: Sofia, Hela, Marya (Marie), Joseph and Bronya. Shortly after this picture was taken, Sofia and Bronya caught typhus fever and Sofia died.

9

for the last time. At the age of thirteen, Marie's oldest sister was dead.

In Marie's short life this was only the first of two immense losses. Two years later tuberculosis took its final toll, and her mother died. Marie was ten.

It took the stricken family a very long time to recover.

Schooldays

During all these difficult years Marie progressed through school with considerable success. Her teachers remembered her well: an unusually intelligent child, two years at least ahead of her classmates, with a powerful memory and an ability to absorb and understand large amounts of information. She would always work very hard and very seriously. They also remembered her as shy, unwilling to push herself forward into people's attention, except when she was fired by the desire to find something out. Then her dogged persistence overcame all obstacles.

Schooldays in Poland then were a difficult time. It was not a happy place, for the Polish people did not rule their own country. For over 100 years, the land had been split and ruled by Austria, Prussia and Russia. In Central Poland, where Marie lived, the so-called King of Poland was in fact the Tsar, the Emperor of Russia, Alexander II.

The Polish people dreamed and organized and prepared again and again to overthrow their Tsarist Russian conquerors and rule the country for themselves. Each time the rebellion was beaten down. Punishment was merciless. Rebels were deported from the country, never to return, and the leaders executed.

During Marie's early childhood, the Russians began introducing new rules designed to keep the Polish people in their control. Little by little they tried to destroy their language and religion. Tsarist officials were moved into all the most important positions in the country and Polish people removed from them. Teachers were allowed neither to give lessons in the Polish language nor to instruct their

pupils in the history or culture of Poland.

How rich the education which Marie, her brother and sisters had at home must have seemed to them! Every Saturday the family gathered by the light of the oil lamp in the warm quiet of their father's study. He would read aloud to them: poetry, stories, history. He translated the great books of different countries from English or French even as he went along. This was how Marie first heard *David Copperfield* by Charles Dickens.

In 1883, when she was 15, Marie emerged from her secondary school with a gold medal to testify to her success. But the future looked very bleak. Women in Poland could not go on to higher education after finishing secondary school studies. They were not taught the subjects needed for entrance to a university or technical school. And so these places were barred to them.

A painting of Warsaw, which shows what it was like when Marie was a child. Poland was under Russian rule and teaching in Polish was against the law. Because she was a girl, Marie was not allowed to go to the university.
(Painting by Bernardo Bellotto.)

Being a boy, Joseph could study to be a doctor. The girls, Marie, Bronya and Hela, had only one choice. If they wanted to continue learning, they would have to go to a university in another country.

But how could they ever do this? As always, the family was desperately short of money. Soon their father would retire, and then there would be only his small pension to sustain the family. Passports, train tickets, food and accommodation would all cost extra. They could never afford to go. They must try to earn a living in Poland as best they could.

But first there came a rare break in the pattern of Marie's life.

Country interlude

Marie was worn out. Her studies and final exams had drained her energies, and an inner sadness had never really left her in the five years since she had lost her mother.

Her father could see the paleness of his youngest daughter and knew something must be done to restore her spirits. He packed her off to relatives in the country. "Rest," he told her. "Enjoy yourself. Come back refreshed."

What idleness! Marie could hardly believe it. There was nothing she *had* to do from one end of the day to the other. She would wake early or late, just as she chose. She could pass the day doing nothing but rolling hoops with her cousins or walking in the woods. She could play games, pick wild strawberries, swim, or read lighthearted novels. She wrote to a schoolfriend, "We swing a lot, swinging ourselves hard and high; we go fishing with torches for shrimps. . . . Sometimes I laugh all by myself, and I contemplate my state of total stupidity with genuine satisfaction." She learned to row and to ride horses.

She began to love the changing seasons of the countryside and its teeming plant and animal life with a passion that never left her. In later life, when unhappiness weighed heavily and the stresses of her life threatened to break her, she always returned to the countryside, drawing her strength and finding

Opposite: Marie's father, with his remaining daughters, from left to right: Marie, Bronya and Hela. This photo was taken shortly before Bronya left to study in Paris.

Marie (standing) and Bronya when they both had jobs as governesses, looking after the children of wealthy families. Both sisters had been saving in the hope that they could go to the Sorbonne in Paris. Bronya had worked hard for several years. It seemed as though they would never succeed, until Marie had the idea of their both saving to send Bronya first. When Bronya qualified as a doctor she would then pay for Marie to join her. The plan worked, but it would mean more years of sacrifice.

again the peace she always felt there.

The blissful year came to an end. Marie was now sixteen. In Warsaw again, she and her sisters had to set about finding some way to earn a living.

It was hardly surprising that their thoughts turned to the profession which they knew so well from their parents, and which they valued very highly – teaching. They began to give private lessons, for a small fee, to the sons and daughters of Warsaw families.

The "great plan"

It was at this time that Marie joined "The Floating University," a rather important-sounding name for a brave group of young people. All over Warsaw, young men and women like Marie were determined to learn the things that were forbidden. As each generation of young Poles had done before them, this generation of energetic, bright young people also nursed a fierce and growing passion: the desire to change their country's future and seize it from the conqueror. They planned to start by educating themselves as best they could – and at any cost. While one of their number kept watch on the streets and at doorways for curious policemen, upstairs, in the attic rooms of private homes, groups of enthusiastic men and women met in secret to listen to lectures, discuss ideas, exchange pamphlets and books, learn of all the new ideas emerging in other countries in Europe. Each knew that if caught, it would mean prison for them all. Yet they continued. Under the influence of this stimulating group, Marie began to yearn to experience these things outside the atmosphere of bleak constraint which the conqueror's laws gave to Poland.

It was now that Marie and Bronya made a very important decision. They *must* go to another country to continue studying. They would not go to Berlin or Petersburg, where Tsarist Russia ruled, but to Paris in France. It seemed to them that knowledge flourished there in a spirit of brilliant freedom which was the summit of their hopes.

Deciding to go was one thing. Getting there was

another. They were earning very little giving private lessons, and it was a thankless, exhausting task. Long hours spent getting across Warsaw in all kinds of weather brought poor results. They could never save enough money that way.

Marie proposed a plan. First, she and Bronya would both work to save enough money to send Bronya to Paris. Then, when Bronya was settled, she would in turn help Marie to save the money for the journey.

Marie made a second, vital decision. Although it meant leaving Warsaw, her family and friends, she would go to work as a governess in the country. The pay would be better than the pittance she got for the private lessons. She was certain that she could save more money this way – and how much faster it would wing them both to the university in Paris!

On the first of January 1886, a dreary winter's day, Marie left for her first country job. She remembered the misery of that day till the end of her life. Ahead of her there lay a strange job and a strange family, for an unknown length of time. Loneliness at the prospect overwhelmed her, and she grew frightened at the gigantic choice she had made.

But she pressed on with that core of obstinate determination which was to be her vital strength in all the years that followed.

The new job was at Szczuki, 60 miles (100 km) north of Warsaw. She found it a strange place, not at all like the countryside she already knew and loved. Her bedroom looked onto the red brick buildings of a smoke-belching sugar factory. All around, the unchanging lines of sugarbeet fields met the eye. Nearby clustered the huts of a small village where peasants and factory workers lived.

The little school on the beet farm

Her employer managed a sugarbeet estate and was part owner of the sugar factory. He lived with his family in a large, old, vine-covered house set amid rambling gardens, orchards, barns and cattlesheds. Here Marie settled in to teach his daughters,

"I have a lively memory of that sympathetic atmosphere of social and intellectual comradeship [at the 'floating university'.] The means of action were poor and the results obtained could not be very considerable; and yet I persist in believing that the ideas that then guided us are the only ones which can lead to sure social progress. We cannot hope to build a better world without improving the individual. Towards this end, each of us must work toward his own highest development, accepting at the same time his share of responsibility in the general life of humanity – our particular duty being to help those to whom we feel we can be most useful."

Marie Curie,
in a letter dated 1924.

Above left: Marie studied in the formally-named "Museum of Industry and Agriculture" on the second floor of this Warsaw building. In fact, this was a name which hid a secret school. Under Russian occupation, Polish people were not allowed their own university and Marie had to learn illegally. Alone in this tiny science laboratory, Marie had her only chance to teach herself how to use scientific experimental equipment.

Above right: This was the country home in Szczuki, Poland, where Marie was governess for three years. She felt very lonely and had to work long hours. By working as a full-time governess, she was able to earn more and could save to help pay for Bronya to go to the science department of the University of Paris to train in medicine.

Bronka – at eighteen as old as Marie herself – and Andzia, ten years old. Marie's duties were not light. For seven hours a day she instructed the daughters and for another hour a day she gave lessons to a workman's son, helping him to prepare for school.

But when she met the peasant children out on the muddy roads one day, she suddenly saw a new task for herself. These children could neither read nor write. They did not go to school at all. They *must,* she decided, be taught: "It is their right. It is what our country needs."

Never mind that once again it would be dangerous, for such teaching would be against the law. It *had* to be done.

Bronka was enthusiastic about the scheme, and wanted to help. Marie's employers agreed. At once the two girls set up the little school in Marie's room in the family house.

The results were slow. But gradually there was immense pleasure as the children began to find that the mysterious marks on paper were no longer so mysterious. After a while parents began to visit the school as well, sitting quietly at the end of the room and watching their children's gleeful progress with unmistakable pride.

Marie now embarked on another equally vital

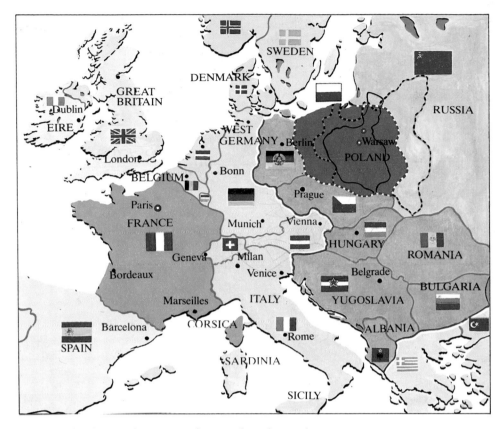

task. In the long winter evenings, when her other duties were finally over for the day, Marie began to educate herself in preparation for the university. In her spacious, quiet room, warmed by a gigantic porcelain stove, she burrowed deep into books about every subject she could obtain – literature, history, sociology and science.

The seeds of her brilliant future life were taking root. She became fascinated most of all by her father's own subjects – physics and mathematics. If there wasn't enough time during the evenings, she would make time by getting up at six o'clock in the morning.

The long wait

At last, in 1885, the sisters reached their first target. They saved enough money to send Bronya to Paris

In 1867, when Marie was born, Poland was divided between Russia, Austria and Prussia (now part of Germany) and did not exist as a country. The black line shows the Russian area, including Warsaw, where she was born.

Following World War I, 1914 1918, the independent Republic of Poland was proclaimed: its borders are shown by the blue/black dotted line. This was overthrown by the German and Russian invasions in 1939 and new frontiers, shown by the red dotted line, were established in 1945 that remain to this day.

17

to study medicine. Marie resigned herself to a long wait. The days and months passed. Enthusiasm for her reading began to falter. She began to feel very alone again; homesickness overwhelmed her, and she began to believe that she would never lead the kind of life she wanted, never attain her dream of going to Paris.

The dream faded, and grew bright, and faded again many times.

"Think of it," she wrote unhappily to her brother Joseph in October of 1888. "I am learning chemistry from a book. You can imagine how little I get out of that, but what can I do, as I have no place to make experiments or do practical work?"

Three long years had passed. Her job at Szczuki came to an end and Marie returned to teaching jobs in Warsaw. Then, unexpected new possibilities opened up. One of her many cousins, Joseph Boguski, directed the "Museum of Industry and Agriculture." This official-sounding name hid another of Poland's secret schools. Inside, there was a small science laboratory, with all the equipment Marie needed.

Losing no time, on Sundays and every free evening she had, Marie began to teach herself to use the apparatus, and to perform simple scientific experiments. She learned to handle the minute amounts of substances and liquids, to measure, weigh, heat, cool and mix them. She observed the action of magnets and gained experience in using the delicate glass tubes, flasks and funnels. Years later she wrote about these early experiences, "From time to time a little unhoped-for success would come to encourage me, and at other times I sank into despair because of the accidents or failures due to my inexperience. But on the whole, even though I learned . . . that progress is neither rapid nor easy, I developed my taste for experimental research during these early trials."

It was the spring of 1890 when the longed-for letter finally arrived from Paris. Bronya, now firmly settled there, was going to marry a fellow medical student. She had passed all her exams with success and only her final exam was still to come. She could

18

now offer her younger sister a home in Paris and urged her to make her final preparations.

It was not until the end of the following year that Marie finally boarded the Paris-bound train. She was nearly 24. Following Bronya's advice she tried to keep her future costs in Paris down by taking everything with her: mattress, blankets, sheets and towels, her few clothes, shoes and hats.

On the platform stood her father, small, elderly, and suddenly very lonely.

"I won't be long," she said. She was certain of that, for her goal was simple – to graduate from the university and return at once to teach in her beloved Poland. "I'll get my degree, and then I'll be back."

As Marie's train steamed slowly out of Warsaw on the journey that would take her more than 800 miles (1400 km) across Europe, the young girl little realized that she was on the threshold of a brilliant

This painting by Jean Beraud shows the kind of street scene of prosperous Paris that would have greeted Marie when she finally arrived there in 1891. She hardly noticed the busy shops but hurried instead to the Sorbonne. When she walked through the great wrought iron gates to register, she knew that the years of toil as a governess had been worthwhile.

new life which would bring her to the notice of the whole world. One of the several bitter losses it would cost her was the fact that she would never again live in Poland.

The Sorbonne

Paris was freedom. Marie could breathe it in the air. Even the murmur of people scurrying along the great boulevards was a song of liberation.

Here people spoke their own language! They read books of their own choice! In the crowded cafés and open-air bookstalls around the university, the hum of conversation seemed to her a vast cauldron in which momentous ideas and new philosophies seethed. Now *she* could be part of this.

Each day she climbed to the upper deck of the horse-drawn bus and rode from her sister's home in the northern suburbs of Paris, over the River Seine to the great cathedral of Marie's dreams – the university of the Sorbonne.

When she first saw it, she stood outside for a long time. How many times she had imagined this moment. She, Marya Sklodowska from Poland, standing in this place that had been a seat of learning for nearly 800 years!

With some 12,000 other students, Marie now had the right to enter these lecture rooms and use these libraries. There was even a place for her in the laboratories of science! The years of lonely struggle in Poland fell away from her. She could see only the future.

But an unexpected shock awaited her. The first lectures were utter misery: she could not understand a word of them! In Poland her French had always seemed quite fluent – fluent enough, at any rate, for her to read widely in the language. But now, lectures on physics, mathematics, chemistry spoken rapidly in French by a *Frenchman* – that was quite another matter.

And then another thing: despite all her reading in Szczuki and Warsaw, she was years behind French students starting these science courses at the Sorbonne. There were vast gaps in her knowledge, chasms of ignorance that she could not simply leap across.

She steeled herself against the disappointment. After all, the years of preparation *had* trained her for one thing: not to be defeated. Learn French, catch up, make good the gaps in her essential knowledge. And do it fast. These were the tasks she set herself, the new mountain she had to climb.

She was utterly determined to do it. She began to spend all her time at the Sorbonne, returning to her sister's home only in the evening. Bronya and her husband, Casimir, were now qualified doctors. They welcomed Marie warmly into their new home. The friendship between the two sisters, which had sustained them through all the years of waiting and planning in Poland, was now stronger than ever. With Casimir, Bronya's husband, Marie struck up a bond of friendship and mutual respect that lasted all their lives.

Nevertheless, it was not many months before the two hours' ride by horse-bus to and from the Sorbonne each day began to take its toll. Marie was very tired by the end of it, and she lost precious study time.

What should be done? The three of them talked it over. Marie felt she should take a room closer to the Sorbonne, in the Latin Quarter, within walking distance of laboratories, libraries and lecture rooms. Bronya and Casimir were reluctant to agree. They knew that the added cost of rent (which she did not have to pay while she lived with them) would drain her small savings. But Marie's certainty convinced them. She started looking for suitable, cheap lodgings. By March of 1892, she had found a room in the Latin Quarter.

Life in a garret

During the years that followed, Marie lived in a succession of tiny rooms, barely furnished and cheap. They provided her with a roof over her head, a place to sleep and study, and that was all she wanted. Like so many thousands of other students, she had just enough money to pay her rent and to buy food and fuel to keep her warm. Often, when it was especially cold, she had to choose – fuel *or* food, not both.

But it did cost very little. And here Marie was able to settle down to her routine of study, study and more study. She worked in the libraries until they closed at 10 o'clock at night, for there was heating and lighting there, and she could save her own skimpy supplies. Sometimes she forgot to eat, or lived on bread, butter and tea for days on end.

When the libraries shut their doors, she returned to her room to read by oil lamp until her eyes could take no more and she fell exhausted into bed.

She walked everywhere, for the horse-bus cost money. But she was always in her place in the front row of lectures, her notebook open and her small, neat hand making careful, detailed, rapid notes. Courses on mathematics, physics, chemistry – she drank them all in. The growing fascination with sciences that had gripped her in Poland now seized her utterly. She was filled with wonder by the mysteries of the natural world as they were unfolded by her lecturers. She was transfixed as these knowledgeable men, their black tailcoats dusty with chalk, expounded their rich fund of knowledge to a rapt audience of students.

This photo of Marie was taken while she was studying for her first degree at the Sorbonne. It shows her simple style of dress which contrasted strongly with the fashionable ladies of Paris. Marie would always dress plainly and practically and would take little interest in what were, to her, irrelevant pleasures.

Her first degree

Marie's first exams drew near, and her whole life now seemed to hang in the balance. All the years of sacrifice and hard work pointed to this hurdle.

A street market in the Latin Quarter of Paris where Marie had found a tiny attic room. She did not mind the poverty, as long as she could study. She also found people who could speak her own language, and she was close to the university. (Painting by Henri-Gaston Darien.)

She took the first exam in July of 1893, when she was 25, eighteen months after her arrival in Paris. When the results were announced, Marie was the top student!

At one and the same time she had learned French and physics, jumped the barriers of missing knowledge, and emerged ahead of all the other students. She was unmistakably a student of exceptional, extraordinary qualities. She had decided not to be satisfied with just one degree and to take a second one the following year, this time in mathematics. Her money worries had unexpectedly lessened, for she was awarded a scholarship from Poland which was given to students who wished to study abroad. It was enough for her to live on for another fifteen months!

By the summer of 1894, within just one year, she passed the exams for a degree in mathematics with distinction, finishing second.

Pierre

That year of 1894 had an even greater importance for Marie. In the early months she had met Pierre Curie, at the home of a Polish friend. She wrote of this moment, "When I came in, Pierre Curie was standing in the window recess near a door leading to the balcony.... I was struck by the expression of his clear gaze.... His rather slow, reflective words, his simplicity, and his smile, at once grave and young, inspired confidence."

So began one of the great partnerships of history. They talked. Marie, at first shyly, but then with a growing confidence, asked Pierre questions about his scientific work. She sought his advice about some problems with her own.

He was astonished by her. Such broad understanding of scientific matters! Such lively interest! Her enthusiasm was infectious, and their conversation became more animated. What an unusual person this young Polish girl was, he thought. He already knew from their mutual friends that she had fought to come to Paris, that she was self-educated and yet had emerged first in the physics exam, the finest among the students. And she seemed to share his own fascination with science. She seemed to feel the same drive to discover the unchanging rules that govern the physical world and to expand her knowledge of them constantly.

It was the beginning of a friendship that was to bring them an immense love, a unique partnership and worldwide fame. Pierre set about trying to persuade Marie to remain in Paris, to marry him, and to begin scientific work together.

Marie swiftly felt a powerful bond of common interest and understanding with this man. He was a scientist already recognized by distinguished scientists in other countries for his brilliant and original work. He was also a gentle, quiet person with great warmth and generosity of nature.

But he was a Frenchman; to stay with him would mean living in France and leaving her beloved Poland and her family for good. It seemed an act of betrayal.

Pierre saw that Marie could not bear the thought

Pierre Curie was thirty-five and already a distinguished scientist and Chief of Laboratories at the Sorbonne when he met Marie in 1894. Being totally devoted to his scientific work, he had never allowed himself the distraction of marriage. But he had reckoned without the bond that grew between him and Marie.

of parting from Poland. He offered instead to go and live and work with her there. Marie knew that in Poland he would not be able to do the work he wanted or live the life he wished. It would be too costly a sacrifice, and he would never be happy.

She wrestled with her own impossible choice: Poland and her family, or Pierre and a scientific partnership that she knew would be something very special. For a whole year she hesitated.

In the end, she chose Pierre. On July 26, 1895, when Marie was 27, they were married. And so Marya Sklodowska from Warsaw became Madame Curie of Paris. It was a name that would, within less than six years, become a household word.

The first years of marriage

Thoughts of future international fame were very far from their minds, however, in those first weeks of an idyllic honeymoon. Now their only preoccupation was to roam the peaceful French countryside on their new bicycles. These were a wedding gift from a relative, and they were to treasure them for many years to come.

In Pierre, Marie had indeed found a fellow spirit. He, too, had always loved the countryside, observed flowers, butterflies, frogs, birds, watched the pattern of the seasons and the cycle of plants and wildlife. Often, in these first years of marriage, they would seize the chance to put their bicycles on a train and make for the woods and fields.

By October Marie and Pierre had settled in a small apartment in Paris and resumed their scientific work. These were busy, peaceful and happy years. They lived quietly with their work, their shared ambitions, and each other. They were now so close in all they did that they even learned to think together. They believed they were better scientists as partners than they would have been alone. Marie was learning a great deal from Pierre, for he had years of experience and knowledge behind him, and he was a fine teacher.

She was given permission to work alongside him in the School of Physics and Chemistry of the City

of Paris where he worked. There he taught his students and at the same time continued with his important research on the structure and growth of crystals. Marie was just beginning her first piece of scientific research.

In September of their third year of marriage, their first child, Irene, was born. Now Marie combined the role of research scientist in the laboratory with wife and mother at home. Little did she realize that this tiny infant would one day follow in the footsteps of her parents and achieve international fame as a pioneering scientist in partnership with a brilliant husband.

Pierre and Marie with their bicycles outside 108 Boulevard Kellermann, Paris, the house they moved to in 1900. They would escape into the countryside on their bicycles on weekends, to relax from the backbreaking work of refining huge quantities of pitchblende.

Within a few months of each other, Marie had produced both her first child, and her first published scientific work – her report on the magnetic properties of steel.

"Doctor of science"

Her next objective was to start working for a doctorate. For this, she would have to find a subject for research that would break new ground in science. She was actually already breaking new ground in merely deciding to do this research, for no woman in the whole of Europe had ever yet completed a doctorate.

Marie's search for a subject began. She started to read reports of the latest experiments by scientists all over the world. One report in particular caught her attention.

It was by a French scientist named Henri Becquerel and had been published the previous year, 1896. Like many scientists of the time, he had been investigating X-rays. These had been discovered only the year before by a German scientist, Wilhelm Röntgen, and they had amazed the world. They were a kind of invisible light which could pass right through thick materials like paper, wood and even metal. Very soon scientists had also discovered that they could pass right through the human body.

This is how they did it. They knew that a photographic film goes dark if it is exposed to any kind of light; the more light it gets, the darker it goes. When they put a photographic film on one side of a person's body and an X-ray machine on the other, the X-rays passed *through* the body and made an image of the shape of the body on the film. The flesh was darker and the bones lighter, because more of the rays passed through the flesh, and less could pass through the bones.

Within days of this discovery, X-rays had been used to find a bullet in a human leg.

Henri Becquerel was one of many scientists working on how X-rays could be put to use. He knew that some chemicals glow when X-rays shine on them. He was trying to find out if other chemicals

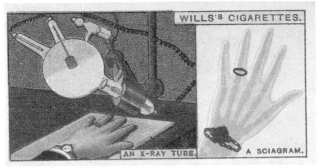

X-RAY APPARATUS POWERED BY A RUHMKORFF COIL, FROM THE "FAMOUS INVENTIONS" AND "DO YOU KNOW?" SERIES OF CIGARETTE CARDS.

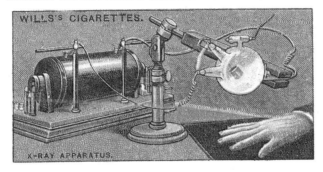

would *send out* X-rays if strong light, like sunlight, was shone on them. One day he had taken a piece of photographic film and wrapped it carefully in several layers of black paper. This was to ensure that no ordinary (visible) light could possibly get through and darken the film, though X-rays *would* be able to pass through. Then he put a metal sheet on top of the wrapped film and sprinkled it with a chemical.

He put the film, the metal sheet and the chemical out in the bright sunlight for a few hours. Then he developed the film to see if the chemical had sent out any rays that had passed through the black paper and the metal and darkened the film. He did the same test with many different chemicals. The only one which had darkened the film had been a chemical called uranium.

But one day there was no sun, so he put his little sandwich of film, metal and uranium in a drawer to wait for the next sunny day. The following days were cloudy. But by some strange stroke of fate,

Becquerel took out the film a few days later and decided to develop it anyway. Unbelievably, the film had the dark shape of the uranium chemical on it! Yet it had been in a dark, locked drawer! No sunlight could *possibly* have reached the uranium and caused it to send out X-rays.

It meant that uranium was giving out some kind of ray *all by itself*. These rays were strong enough to pass through the metal sheet and the black paper and reach the photographic film, just like X-rays. But from other tests he did, he realized they were not the same thing at all!

Becquerel had discovered radioactivity. (We also call it radiation.) At the time, all he knew was that here was some kind of miraculously powerful ray, quite invisible to the eye and hitherto totally unknown to the world.

So he had his report published. But no one had yet taken up the challenge to find out what these rays were and where they came from, not even Becquerel himself.

Marie became more and more fascinated by the possibilities. What questions there were to answer!

Work on radioactivity begins

Marie had found her subject for research. She was given a tiny room, used partly as a store room, at the School of Physics and Chemistry. It was icy cold, damp and altogether inhospitable. The discomfort was unpleasant enough, but far more importantly, the cold made it extremely difficult for her equipment to work accurately.

Her first step was to find a way of measuring how strong these mysterious Becquerel rays were – the rays given out by uranium. Marie had the perfect machine to do this. It had been invented by Pierre and his brother Jacques and was called an electrometer. It could measure electrical currents in air, no matter how tiny they were.

Becquerel had already shown that uranium rays caused an electrical current to flow through the air. So Marie could measure the strength of the rays by measuring the strength of the electrical current

Rozwijać pracownie naukowe, które Pasteur nazwał „świętemi przybytkami ludzkości", – ułatwiać zadanie tym, co pracują dla nauki, – otaczać opieką młodzież pragnącą wiedzy, aby pozyskiwać pracowników przyszłości, – stwarzać warunki, w którychby wrodzone a cenne zdolności mogły się uświadamiać i posłużać służbie ideału, – jest to prowadzić społeczeństwo drogą rozwoju potęgi, tak duchowej jak materyalnej.

Marya Skłodowska Curie

that they caused in the air. Quickly she obtained as many samples of metals and minerals as she could; then she tested them all.

Within days, she had her first result. She found that the strength of the rays depended *only* on the amount of uranium in the samples: the more uranium there was, the stronger were the rays. The strength of the rays was not changed by whatever else it was mixed with or whether the substance she was testing was wet or dry, powdered or in lumps, hot or cold. Only the amount of uranium in it was important.

Rays from anywhere else?

Uranium is what is known as a *chemical element*. Scientists had given this name to the basic materials or substances from which *all other* materials in the world are made. They are substances like gold, silver, iron, copper, carbon, sulphur, oxygen, hydrogen and chlorine. At the time Marie was beginning her work on uranium rays, scientists knew of about 83 elements.

Marie knew that uranium gave off the rays. The

This is part of a letter from Marie to her sister, Bronya. It is one of many examples of her writing showing her lifelong dedication to service to mankind through science. "To develop science laboratories – which Pasteur called 'holy shrines of humanity' – to facilitate the tasks of those who work for science, to extend care over the young who thirst for knowledge – and thus to gain workers of the future – to create conditions in which innate and precious talents may be realized and devoted to the service of ideals … this is the way to lead society along the path of developing its power, both spiritual and material."

next question she asked was: do any other elements give off the same kind of rays?

She tested all the chemical elements. Now she had her second important result: one other element, named thorium, gave out rays like those of uranium. Tested by her electrometer, they seemed to be just as strong.

Obviously it was no longer enough to call these rays "uranium rays." A more general name had to be found. It was now that Marie began to use the word "radioactivity," and this is the name we still use today.

Into the unknown

By now Marie had answered the basic question that most research workers would have asked: which substances give off these strange rays? She now knew that only *two* elements did so. Where to next?

Marie's instincts as a true explorer were now crucial. She was curious; she simply wanted to throw her net as far and wide as she could and see what she came up with. She set about obtaining samples of all kinds of natural materials – minerals, rocks, sand – and she tested them all with her electrometer.

If her first results had been right, she thought, then only the samples that contained some uranium or thorium would be radioactive. If they did *not* contain uranium or thorium, then they would *not* be radioactive.

This turned out to be quite true. So Marie put aside all the samples that were not radioactive. She turned her attention to the radioactive ones.

She measured the radioactivity of each one in turn. Then came the totally unexpected, dramatic result. The samples with uranium and thorium in them gave off rays that were *far, far stronger* than could be caused by the amount of uranium or thorium! When they tested a mineral called pitch-blende, for example, it was *four times* more radio-active than chemicals that they had tested that contained *the same amount* of uranium!

Perhaps she had made a mistake? She did the

Opposite: Radium is a highly radioactive substance; it also gives off a radioactive gas called radon. Marie's shed in the Rue Lhomond in Paris was badly ventilated and she had no protection against radiation.

It was Marie's discoveries about radiation that led to a completely new area of science: nuclear physics. To generate power by nuclear fission, you must split uranium atoms into their component parts. The first picture shows the structure of a simple atom. The next shows how, when an atom disintegrates, the protons and neutrons form one sort of radiation, the electrons form another, while gamma rays are produced by the disintegration itself. The last picture shows what resistance various materials can give to the three different sorts of radiation.

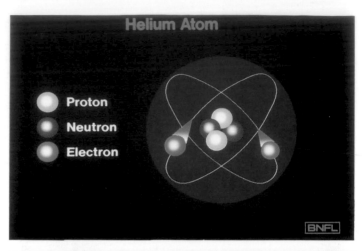

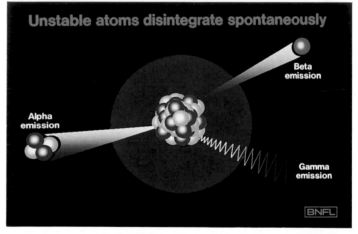

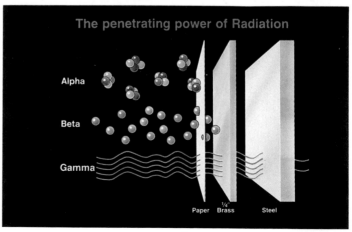

This is pitchblende ore. Marie's experiments made her realize that pitchblende contained a new, highly-radioactive element. But the separation of the minute amounts of radium took her four years of exhausting work to <u>prove</u> what she already knew.

experiment again, twice, three times . . . ten, twenty times. Each time, the result was the same. There was no mistake.

And what was more, the strength of the radiation was extraordinary! Where on earth did it come from?

There could be only one explanation. There must be *something else* in the pitchblende that was much more radioactive than uranium and thorium. But it must be there in a minute quantity – for no one had ever noticed it before.

The possibility that sprang to her mind then could hardly be believed. She had already tested every one of the elements that scientists *already knew about.* Could she have found a *new* element?

The task before her now assumed great importance. If there really was a new element there, an element with extraordinary radioactivity, then it was a discovery of great significance for the world.

On the track of radium

Marie now entered a period of time when her work was a supreme effort of faith in her own knowledge and judgment. She had no doubt that she was on

Above and right: Marie could not find premises to conduct her research. Finally, she was allowed to use this abandoned, leaking shed. She worked here in appalling conditions for almost four years.

News of her vital scientific work became known to scientists all over the world and a famous German chemist, Wilhelm Ostwald, came to see for himself. He was shocked to see the "laboratory" and said, "It was a cross between a stable and a potato-cellar, and, if I had not seen the worktable with the chemical apparatus, I would have thought it a practical joke."

the track of a new, powerfully radioactive element. But other scientists doubted it. They were sure she had simply made a mistake in her measurements.

Marie knew she had made no mistakes, but she had to prove it. She had to find the unknown substance, see it, and show it to everyone else.

Pierre had been watching all her efforts so far with equal excitement. Now, in the early summer of 1898, he decided to put aside his own work on crystals and join Marie in her search for the unknown element.

They would look for it in pitchblende ore. They knew which elements were already in pitchblende. So if they separated out all these known elements and removed them, one by one, what they had left would be the new element. What they couldn't know was that it would be like looking for one *particular* grain of sand in a mountain of grains!

In fact, Marie and Pierre had discovered not one, but two new elements. By July of 1898, they were able to confirm the existence of one, which they named polonium, after Poland. But all their evidence pointed to another, still hidden. By the end of 1898, they were absolutely certain of the second, and they named it radium. Polonium never had the same importance as radium, for it was radium's gigantic radioactivity which was to open doors into a whole new realm for the scientists of the twentieth century.

Marie and Pierre had guessed that, because the new element had not been noticed by anyone before, it must be present in the pitchblende in very tiny amounts. If they were to extract enough of it from the ore to *prove* its existence, they would need very large amounts of pitchblende.

In the end, a factory in Austria that extracted uranium from pitchblende for use in the manufacture of glass let the Curies have the pitchblende waste after the uranium had been removed.

The next problem was where to work. They would need space to work with several tons of ore. Marie's little store-room would never do! They had no money to buy or rent facilities and began to wonder if they would ever solve the problem. But

"It is true that the discovery of radium was made in precarious conditions: the shed which sheltered it seems clouded in the charms of legend. But this romantic element was not an advantage: it wore out our strength and delayed our accomplishment. With better means, the first five years of our work might have been reduced to two, and their tension lessened."

Pierre Curie.

Right: The electroscope with ionization chamber which was used by Marie Curie in her experiments. It had originally been designed by Pierre Curie and his brother Jacques to measure tiny currents of electricity. It was never used until Marie needed it for her research.

they managed to persuade the principal of the School of Physics to let them use an old abandoned shed in the school yard. It was no more than a wooden shack, lit by a dingy skylight, with a leaky roof and a beaten earth floor. In the summer they would suffocate with heat. In the winter they would freeze. The only advantage was that they could use the yard for work that produced poisonous fumes and let the wind blow the gases away. Their equipment was some old pine tables, some furnaces and burners, and Pierre's electrometer.

How they found radium

The day came when a heavy wagon drew up outside and deposited the great sackloads of pitchblende ore. This is what they had to do. First, they took

a sample of pitchblende and sifted it to remove any rubbish. Then they ground it and boiled it with soda so that it separated into a solid material and a liquid. Then they discarded the liquid.

Next the solid material had to be dissolved in acid. Now the solution had to be treated with different chemicals in order to separate the elements they did not want and discard them. So began an endless process of mixing, dissolving, heating, filtering, distilling, crystallizing, on and on and on. Each time they removed an element, Pierre measured it *and* what was left with the electrometer. As the portion they worked with got smaller and smaller, its radioactivity got bigger and bigger. The radioactivity of Marie's radium was going to be enormous!

Day in, day out, they were at the laboratory. Sackful after sackful was patiently reduced to a thimbleful of radium. And then on to the next sackful. Marie lifted and poured the great cauldrons of fuming liquids. Sometimes, for hours at an end, she stirred it with an iron bar almost as big as herself.

They started the process of extracting pure radium from pitchblende in 1899. It took them four years of hard work, determination and dedication. It had to be done with painstaking care, for they could make no mistakes.

They were often in a state of total exhaustion,

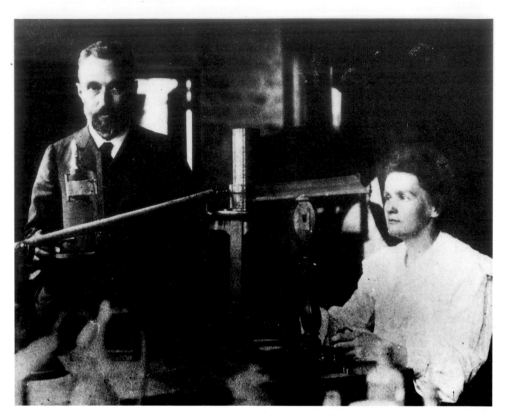

Pierre worked constantly at Marie's side during the years of her most tiring research. He recognized the importance of her work and gave up his own to help her in the long battle to prove that radium actually existed.

such was the mammoth scale of their unending task. The shed and yard were filled with the stench of chemicals. Sometimes they were in depair because of accidents. Wind blew iron and coal dust into the purified radium products, and Marie had to start again. Or a dish was spilled on the floor or the bench, and months of patient work were lost in a sodden pool at their feet.

Victory

In 1902, when Marie was 35, and 45 months after the day on which the Curies first announced that radium *probably* existed, Marie finally won her battle. She prepared a tenth of a gram of *pure radium*. Now the world could actually see it!

But already scientists were buzzing with news of Marie's discovery. A great competition had begun to be the first to use radium to discover as much as possible about radioactivity. Even as Marie continued with the work of purifying radium, Pierre had been studying it and getting to know it better. He found out a number of very important things, among them the fact that other substances placed near radium actually became radioactive themselves! This is what we call *induced radioactivity*.

During this period of exhausting work, Marie and Pierre also managed to produce a document of tremendous scientific significance. It was a summary of all the work and knowledge about radioactive substances at that time.

The science of radioactivity was now developing so fast that Marie and Pierre realized they needed people to help them. It was now that scientists of the finest quality began to collect around the Curies, developing their work in other areas, even before radium had been purified.

Throughout these years, their baby daughter, Irene, was growing older. She was looked after during the day by Pierre's father. In the evening, Marie would return home to the tasks of a mother – bathing, feeding and playing with the little girl, reading her stories and sitting with her in the dark, until she fell asleep.

And sometimes, when the baby finally slept and the evening's household duties were over, they would leave Irene for a short while in the care of her grandfather and return to the laboratory. There they would stand in the dark and look at the soft glow of their radium, beautiful as Pierre had said he hoped it would be. Their partnership had never been so complete and so satisfying as in these four years in that ramshackle shed.

Radium tells all

At the turn of this century, scientists believed that they understood the structure of matter. They knew that all materials in the world are formed from chemical elements, and they thought that all elements were made up of building blocks that they called *atoms*. As far as they knew, the atom was the smallest piece of matter.

"The first result to emerge was that the activity of the uranium compounds depended only on the amount of uranium present…. In scientific terms, this is the most important single piece of work carried out by Marie Curie. What she had shown was that the radiation … has a different origin and must come from the atom itself…. From this simple discovery, twentieth-century science was able to elucidate the structure of the atom."

Robert Reid, from his biography, "Marie Curie."

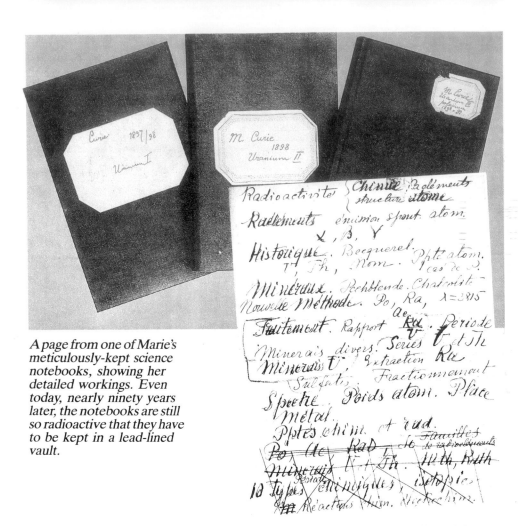

A page from one of Marie's meticulously-kept science notebooks, showing her detailed workings. Even today, nearly ninety years later, the notebooks are still so radioactive that they have to be kept in a lead-lined vault.

In 1900 Marie had the idea that radioactivity was not caused by something acting on a substance from outside it, but by something going on *inside* the substance's atoms. Perhaps, she reasoned, there were minute agitating particles within the atom?

She never herself investigated this idea any further. Yet other scientists did, and within the next ten years the secrets of the structure of matter were revealed. Marie's radium, and her idea about the source of radioactivity, were the keys that finally unlocked the closed door.

From then on, the course by which scientists reached their revolutionary knowledge was extraordinarily rapid. Even as Marie worked at purifying radium, others were exploring its rays. What happened if you put a magnet near them? Did they affect air, other gases, solid substances or liquids? How powerful was the extraordinary heat given off by radium? They learned, too, that it made any substance near it become radioactive.

By the end of 1899, all this work in Germany, Austria and France produced a sudden burst of simultaneous discovery. In France, Pierre had realized that there were two kinds of radium rays.

Work on the atom

Many thousands of miles away in Canada, a scientist named Ernest Rutherford was reading about the work of the Curies, Becquerel and others, and adding their results to his own.

One of his experiments with uranium rays had already produced results matched by Pierre's with radium. Rutherford also discovered there were two kinds of rays. He named them *alpha* and *beta* rays.

Rutherford also discovered that when he blew air across a radioactive substance, a radioactive gas was formed. He named it the *emanation*. Any substance that came into contact with the emanation in turn became radioactive.

Rutherford was later joined in his work by an English scientist named Frederick Soddy. There came the thrilling day when this brilliant pair finally realized exactly what was happening: when a substance gave out radiation, its atoms were *breaking up*. Alpha and beta rays were actually particles of the atom shooting out as it disintegrated!

As their work continued, they were able to build up a clearer and clearer picture of how the atom is constructed. By 1911 Rutherford had developed a picture very similar to the one we have today. Modern science was now well on the path to the release and harnessing of the enormous energy stored within this minute powerhouse.

And all of this came about because young Marie Curie had thrown her radium into the pool of scientific effort. It was more than a million times more

"The Curies could have made a fortune if they had patented their process for producing radium but, poor as they were, they did not wish to take personal advantage of their discovery. They revealed their secrets to the world in the interests of humanity, and a method was devised for treating cancer patients with radium."

Norman Wymer, from "The Inventors."

radioactive than uranium. The ripples from her discovery would lead, in a direct line of descent, to the dawn of the nuclear age.

These early workers, particularly Rutherford and Becquerel, had much to thank Marie personally for. So much of their work had been unsuccessful or disappointingly slow until she sent them powerful samples of radium to use in their experiments.

A miracle cure?

As early as 1900, radium had revealed another great secret. Two German scientists found that the substance had significant effects on the human body.

Pierre Curie and Becquerel made similar discoveries; both had tested the effect of radium on skin. Pierre strapped a sample of impure radium to his arm for ten hours. The skin became red, as though burned. After several days it developed scabs, then a wound which needed dressing. When the skin had finally healed *52 days later*, there was still a scar. Marie had also carried a tiny amount

Marie and Pierre, with Henri Becquerel, received the Nobel Prize for Physics for their research into radioactivity. The Nobel Prize brought the Curies world fame and respect, but the quiet, reticent couple hated the publicity and demands on their time, as it interfered with their continuing research.

of radium in a sealed glass tube inside a metal container. She had similar burns.

By 1903 Pierre had collaborated with two French doctors in testing the action of radium on diseased animals. Amazingly, radium destroyed the diseased cells. Could it therefore cure abnormal growths, such as cancer? Further tests suggested that it would.

The miracles that radium could perform must have seemed unending. Now, with these tests, a whole new possibility emerged: a cure for cancer victims. French doctors made the first treatments of diseased people with success, using tubes of radium emanation supplied by Marie and Pierre. The new techniques of cancer treatment became known as Curietherapy.

It was clear now that radium would be needed on a very large scale to supply cancer therapy. Factories were required. And so a new industry was born.

Marie and Pierre observed its growth with pride.

Doctor of science

Meanwhile, Marie prepared her thesis for her doctoral examination. It was ready by June 25, 1903: a long and comprehensive summary of radioactivity since she, with her radium, had generated the immense burst of investigation by scientists. How much had happened since she had first chosen to study Becquerel's strange rays!

The university examiners interrogated her closely, watched by a large audience of scientists, friends and members of Marie's and Pierre's families. Marie answered all questions with quiet certainty. Her grasp of this new subject was clearly immense. It surpassed that of all others in the room, including her examiners. And *she* was the motivating force behind the avalanche of knowledge that she so clearly laid before them. They awarded her a doctoral degree "with great distinction." Marie was the first woman in Europe ever to receive one.

Before the year was over, there would be the crowning glory to their success. In December, Marie

"It might even be thought that radium could become very dangerous in criminal hands, and here the question can be raised whether mankind benefits from knowing the secrets of Nature, whether it is ready to profit from it or whether this knowledge will not be harmful for it.... I am one of those who believe with Nobel that mankind will derive more good than harm from the new discoveries."

Pierre Curie,
Nobel Lecture, June 6, 1905.

and Pierre won the most important international scientific prize. Jointly with Becquerel, who had first discovered the miracle rays, Marie and Pierre were awarded the Nobel Prize for Physics.

Made ill by radium

But the Curies were not well enough to travel to Sweden to receive the prize and give the Nobel Lecture on their work. Radium, the miracle cure, was beginning to exact a crippling toll on its discoverers. Early on, Pierre had written to a friend that Marie was "always tired, without being exactly ill." An overwhelming, continual, listless fatigue seemed to have overtaken them. Over the four years purifying radium, Marie had lost fourteen pounds in weight. For some time Pierre had been suffering from what the doctors called "rheumatism," bouts of extreme pain in his legs so bad that he had to stay in bed for whole days at a time, weak from the agony and the trembling. At times his hands were too painful to write properly, and he had difficulty dressing himself.

We now know that air made radioactive by radioactive substances causes severe breathing disorders among radium workers who do not protect themselves properly. These emanations drifted freely around Marie and Pierre's laboratory. We also know now that radiation from gamma rays causes serious damage to the bone marrow where our bodies manufacture our blood. Many cancerous diseases are caused by these gamma rays. By 1903 all the worst symptoms of what we now know as radiation sickness were already present in Marie and Pierre.

Rutherford visited them on the evening they celebrated Marie's degree. Pierre did his usual party trick: he pulled a small tube of radium from his pocket and allowed it to glow softly in the dark for the wonderment of his guests. But Rutherford saw how the ends of his fingers were red and sore, as though burned. The tube shone like a beacon to Marie's success. It also beckoned with fatal dangers. None of them yet recognized the severity of the

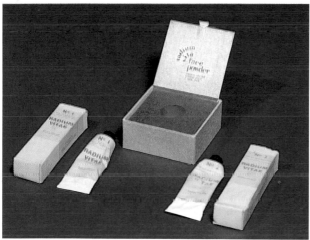

Above: Radium and radioactivity became the rage after Marie and Pierre's Nobel Prize was awarded. No one yet realized the danger as many quack remedies and gimmicky products reached the market. These "sparklets" for making soda water contained radon gas – goodness knows what it did to the insides of the people who drank it!

Left: Radium Vita face powder from the 1920s. Women who used this were liable to develop cancer. Workers in the watch industry who painted luminous watch hands with radioactive paint were told to lick the brushes to keep the tips fine. Many later died of a cancerous condition known as "radium jaw."

threat, that radium would be permanently destructive to the body. For the moment their chief worry was the problems it caused with the accuracy of their equipment.

The price of fame

Marie Curie was now internationally famous. Everyone had heard of the discoveries of this hitherto obscure Polish woman. The story of her mammoth effort in that grim shed in Paris captured the imagination of people throughout Europe and America. Such determination! Such energy and brilliance! And from a woman! For Marie had entered a field of work in which it was very unusual for a woman to succeed. Most people assumed that women would not be able to understand it so well or to make the same effort as men. Most women of the time would not even try to prove otherwise. Yet this woman had taken on the challenge and proved herself to be not merely equal, but one of the most exceptional.

A cure for cancer

What also captured the public imagination and shot Marie to fame was the future possibility of a cancer cure. *She* had made it possible. It was *her* radium that gave the wonder cure. The world longed to see and thank her.

Tragically, this intense wish to acknowledge Marie had, as Marie herself described it, "all the effects of a disaster" for the Curies. They were quiet, private people. They wanted simply to get on with their work, enjoy their family and friends, and little more. Within days of winning the Nobel Prize, this was no longer possible.

The Curies began to live a life of siege, unable to move for fear of the next intrusion into their lives. They cringed beneath these attacks on their privacy and never got used to the public acclaim. "Never have we been less at peace," Pierre wrote. "There are days when we have hardly any time to breathe."

Yet throughout it all they continued to be unswervingly generous with all information about radium and the process for separating it from pitchblende. They would keep no secrets. They believed that knowledge should be disseminated freely and as rapidly as possible for the benefit of science and humanity. Working from the detailed techniques which the Curies described, whole industries were set up in Europe and America, and these industries would make vast sums of money for the men who founded them.

"If our discovery has a commercial future, that is an accident by which we must not profit. And radium is going to be of use in treating disease.... It seems impossible to take advantage of that."

Marie Curie and Pierre Curie discussing whether to patent radium, from "Madame Curie" by Eve Curie.

Despite the constant interruptions, Marie and Pierre struggled to continue work. The year 1904 was particularly exhausting, for Marie was pregnant again. She was very ill this time. Bronya came from Poland to help and was shocked by her younger sister's condition. She seemed at her lowest ebb. The continual sense of ill health, which Marie and Pierre still did not link with their work, and the effects of fame took a heavy toll.

In December 1904, when Marie was 37, a second daughter, Eve, was born. She was healthy and robust, and her antics began to bring new life into the tired woman. She began to feel lighter and freer than she had for some time, and the rest after having the baby renewed her energies.

In the latter part of that year, a professorship was specially created at the Sorbonne for Pierre. Marie was made his laboratory chief. For the first time since she had started her scientific work, she would be getting a salary! And now they could move out of the shed into a proper laboratory at the Sorbonne.

Now Marie divided her time between the laboratory and teaching two days a week at a girls' school near Versailles. She had begun this work in 1900

In 1900, Marie Curie was appointed physics lecturer at a girls' school in Sèvres, near Paris. Both she and Pierre were forced to take teaching jobs to bring in extra money. The plan was successful but it robbed them of precious time during a vital research period. Marie is shown here with her graduation class of 1904. She was the first woman to be appointed as a lecturer at this school.

because they needed the money. But with characteristic commitment, she had introduced revolutionary changes, beginning to teach *practical* science to the young girls. They would work with Marie not just from books, but with their hands.

Pierre's rheumatism continued to mar their lives. The bouts of pain were so intense that sometimes he moaned right through the night, watched over anxiously by Marie.

The dreadful year

Easter of 1906 brought a welcome holiday. The weather was warm, and Pierre relaxed with Marie and the two children. In country woods and fields, surrounded by the early growth of spring, he felt better. Eve, now fourteen months old, kept them laughing as she tottered along the muddy tracks after butterflies.

But back in Paris, the weather closed in, wet and dreary and cold. One Thursday afternoon in April, Pierre set off for a working lunch with university colleagues. Marie was to see him later at the laboratory. After lunch he shook hands with everyone, put his umbrella up and walked out into the rain.

It was the last time anyone saw him alive. In the driving rain of that grim afternoon, he had tried to cross a busy road, crowded with carts and trams and cars. Within seconds he was dead, crushed beyond recognition beneath the heavy wheels of a horse-wagon.

When they brought Marie the news, she retired into a white-faced, icy silence. Eve, in the book she later wrote about her mother, tells how Marie went out into the wet garden and sat, her elbows on her knees, her head on her hands, as though waiting for the companion who would never return.

Only those close to Marie knew that from this moment on, she felt unbearably and incurably lonely. Half her life was cut from her in one stroke – the man with whom she had shared and planned everything.

Yet there were decisions to make. Eve and Irene

"It is impossible for me to describe the meaning and depth of this turning point in my life, as a result of the loss of him who was my closest companion and friend. Crushed by the blow, I was unable to think of the future. And yet, I could not forget what my husband sometimes said that even without him I should work on."

Marie Curie.

Marie with her two daughters, Irene and Eve. This photograph was taken shortly after Pierre's death and shows how abandoned and vulnerable the little family felt. Irene worked with Marie at a very early age and she went on to develop the research on radioactivity. This would lead to the third Nobel Prize for the Curies.

needed her and she must continue to give them a warm, loving home, make up for the loss of their father, provide an income for them, ensure their education.

The university wrestled with the questions of how to help and who should succeed to Pierre's vacant professorship. It became clear that there was only one scientist capable of doing the work Marie and Pierre had begun and only one teacher worthy of following Pierre – Marie herself. Traditions and customs that did not allow for a woman's ever becoming a professor must be swept aside.

As the summer wore on, Marie gradually found a new focus, preparing her lectures for the Sorbonne. She *must* do justice to Pierre, and to herself, and to the richness of their work together.

Her first lecture in November 1906, caused a sensation. For the first time ever, a woman was going to speak at the Sorbonne! And more – the

"Today has seen 'the celebration of a victory for feminism.' If a woman is allowed to teach advanced studies to both sexes, where afterwards will be the pretended superiority of man? I tell you, the time is near when women will become human beings."

"Le Journal," on Marie Curie's first lecture in the Sorbonne, November 6, 1906.

Opposite: After Pierre's death in 1906, Marie was bereft. But she threw herself into further research and worked tirelessly to give other scientists research opportunities. She was determined to isolate radium and polonium as pure salts and she earned a second Nobel Prize – the only person ever to achieve it twice.

woman was Madame Curie, benefactor of humanity! An hour and a half before the lecture began, the hall was already packed to bursting point. Scientists and students flocked in, but so did men and women of fashion, society people, curious onlookers and journalists.

She began the lecture at the exact point where Pierre had finished all those months ago.

Marie's life's work

In the years after she lost Pierre, Marie began to carve a new purpose to her existence – a central aim that formed the core of all her efforts, and one that had been as dear to Pierre's heart as to her own. She prepared to found a school of radioactivity and to create a team of scientists who would be able to push the world's knowledge of the subject ever further.

It would be many years before the idea came to fruition, however. In the meantime, there was much that needed her attention. She continued teaching at the girls' school. At the Sorbonne she gave the world's first course on radioactivity. She collected all Pierre's work and published it. Then she did the same with her own: two massive works of reference.

In the laboratory, she developed a way of measuring the purity and strength of radium preparations. It was critically important work, not least of all for therapists preparing doses for the treatment of cancerous diseases.

In 1911, at the age of 44, Marie Curie was awarded the Nobel Prize for the second time, this time in chemistry. She was the first person ever to receive the award twice.

In 1912, the Sorbonne and the famous Pasteur Institute for Medical Research decided to found a Radium Institute in Paris. It would be built in the newly-named Rue Pierre Curie and would be devoted to research in radioactivity and Curietherapy. For almost ten years now, cancerous growths had been treated by radium rays; recently there had been some spectacular successes.

Building began in 1913. Now a dark-clothed,

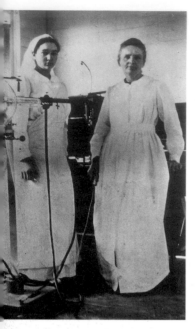

Above: Marie and Irene
Curie spent World War I
helping to X-ray wounded
men. When Marie started
this work, the French Army
possessed only one mobile
X-ray car. Marie knew what
a vital role X-rays could play
in dealing with wounded
men. She personally
organized the conversion of
200 vehicles, known as
"Little Curies," that were
able to function on the war
front. She also established
over 50 X-ray posts. Her
work enabled more than a
million injured men to
receive treatment.

serious little figure could frequently be seen tramping through the building site. Marie personally supervised the garden, choosing trees and planting roses. This must be the perfect home for radio-activity, long, long after she was gone!

But when all was finally ready, there was no one left to work there. The First World War had begun.

Marie's war work

Everyone had offered themselves for war work. Marie's decision was swift. There was one obvious task she could perform. Instinct told her the war would be a long one, and numbers of soldiers would have shattered limbs and terrible wounds from bomb fragments and bullets. The army would need X-ray units to deal with these injuries. But there were very few in France and none at the battlefront.

This, then, would be her task, to set up mobile, light X-ray units that could travel *to* the wounded men. And she would train people to use them. Although she had never worked with X-rays, she knew a great deal about them, so she would have to teach herself.

Within ten days of her decision, she was touring Paris, asking people for supplies. From wealthy citizens she obtained money and vehicles. From makers of scientific equipment, university departments, scientific laboratories, she gradually obtained all the apparatus she would need. Then she persuaded car makers to convert the vehicles into X-ray ambulances. She drew volunteers to work with her from among professors, scientists and engineers.

By late October of 1914, the first mobile X-ray unit rolled to the battlefront. It was an ordinary car, carrying an X-ray machine driven by a generator off the engine, curtains and some screens, and gloves for the operators to protect their hands from the rays. On board were Marie, a doctor, two assistants and a driver-mechanic. One of the assistants was Irene, now 17, and just beginning her own brilliant career alongside her mother.

The first wounded man they handled had bullets

in arm, hip and brain, as well as bomb splinters and fractures all over him. It was a terrible shock to them both. Swiftly they had to place him in front of the machine and search out the position of all the bullets and fragments of bombs. By the end of that first day they had X-rayed 30 men. Before long it was thousands, and in the last two years of the war, more than a million men passed through Marie's X-ray posts – the 20 mobile cars and 200 more units in the military hospitals.

Marie had never done anything by halves – now she had trained herself to use the equipment, learned human anatomy, taught herself to drive a car and mastered basic car mechanics. She had to sleep anywhere and eat anything as she went constantly from the teaching in Paris to the 400 French and Belgian hospitals at the front. The only thing that kept her from her work were the bouts of her recurring, exhausting, and still unexplained illness.

The landscape was flattened during World War I as men in trenches fought over the same territory for months and years on end. Such horrific casualties had never been seen in any previous war and nine million men were killed. This picture is of an advanced Red Cross dressing-station during the Battle of Pozieres Ridge in 1916. It shows the muddy conditions Marie Curie endured. She was content to go without meals and forgo a comfortable bed. She seemed happy to endure years of hardship as long as she could help.

Marie Curie has appeared on stamps from several countries.

Below: A postcard commemorating the fiftieth anniversary of Marie's death: July 4, 1984.

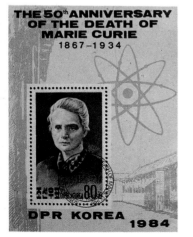

She also began to think about how her own radium could help the war effort. By 1915 doctors were already using it to treat scar tissue, arthritis and other diseases. They also found that the emanation from radium, called *radon,* was a useful source of curing rays.

Now Marie also began to provide tubes of radon for a radium therapy service for all the hospitals.

The Institute finally begins

When the war came to an end, Marie continued to teach X-ray techniques for two more years. But the Radium Institute could now begin to serve its original purpose.

The trouble was that in a war-torn France there were few resources to be had. Marie needed equipment and money for the scientific work. And she needed radium.

Since she had discovered it, the price of radium had rocketed. In 1903, Marie had given her radium from four years of hard work to other scientists. It had steadily risen in price and during the war when it had been used in therapy and for gunsights and compass cards because of its luminous glow, the price had reached an all-time high.

Marie had made her own radium available for Curietherapy. Now she desperately needed radium for her own research scientists to work with. And she, its discoverer, had no money to buy it with!

Help came from an unexpected source. An American journalist named Marie Meloney invited her to go to the United States on a fund-raising tour. America, Marie Meloney declared, would give her the radium she needed.

Marie shrank from the prospect. But how else could she get the radium? Reluctantly, she agreed. But she took her two daughters, Eve, now 16, and Irene, 23, with her for help and support.

The tour was a huge success. America greeted Marie with all the warmth, pomp and ceremony it could muster. Flag-waving, singing crowds greeted her everywhere. Everyone wanted to see this person who had enriched the world with her discovery, and whose story of resolute effort had so captured the public imagination. In May, 1921, the President of the United States presented Marie Curie with the precious gram of radium.

But the strain of the journey was too much for her. Exhausted and very ill, she collapsed and was unable to complete the planned tour. Yet she returned to Paris richer in more than radium. She now understood how she could attract interest, money and resources for radium work. If so, then she had no choice. As long as she was strong enough, she would steel herself to make these kinds of tours. And so began a period in which Marie's richest work was as creator, teacher and supporter of the efforts of others. Inspired, nurtured and guided by her, the team she gathered at the institute would, in time, reveal some of the most important secrets of radioactivity.

Another Curie triumph

In 1934 her life culminated in a new pinnacle of achievement. Irene had by now married one of Marie's most gifted scientists, Frédéric Joliot. This pair, so like Marie and Pierre four decades before, were now in the forefront of the attempt to reveal the innermost workings of the atom. In January of 1934, they made a discovery as important as Marie and Pierre's discovery of radium over 30 years before. They found that by bombarding some metals with radioactive rays, they could change the metal into a *new* radioactive substance, *not known in nature.* They had discovered *artificial* radioactivity. Now a new door to the future was open. In time scientists would be making radioactive substances specifically produced for innumerable purposes in modern science, industry, agriculture and medicine. In 1935 this work would win Irene and Frédéric the Nobel Prize – the third to go to the Curie family.

Meanwhile, at the Institute, her colleague, Professor Regaud, continued the unending war against cancer. Between the end of the war and 1935 over 8,000 patients were cared for there. Doctors flocked to the Institute from all over the world

Above: Marie Curie received eight prizes and sixteen medals.

Below: The statue of Marya Sklodowska-Curie standing in front of the Cancer Research Institute in Warsaw. The institute is named after her.

Marie and other distinguished scientists attending the Council of Physique Solvay in Brussels, early in 1911. Marie was the only woman to attend.

to learn the techniques developed there.

In this year of success, however, Marie was precariously close to the end of her lifetime's work. For over a decade now, she had suffered from painful humming in her ears. She was also nearly blind, even though doctors had operated several times on cataracts in her eyes. We now know these are early symptoms of radiation sickness. She often became dizzy and weak, as though she had bad influenza.

Elsewhere the crippling cost of radium had become tragically apparent. In the early 1920s, several workers in a London hospital died from exposure to radium. Many thousands of laboratory workers all over Europe and America were showing horrifying effects. An American dentist had found cancer of the jaw in workers who painted luminous numbers on clocks and watches. They had been licking their paint brushes to a fine point and receiving radiation from the radium-based paint. There were scores of other horrors, caused by dishonest people pretending to be doctors and selling beauty creams and bogus medicines made from radium.

One day in May 1934, Marie began to feel particularly ill. She left some work unfinished, telling her scientists that she would go home to rest and return soon to finish it with them. She walked around the garden, worrying about the rambler rose. It looked sick and needed urgent care. Then she went home.

She never left her bed again. Test after test was performed on her, but doctors could still not name the disease. Suspecting tuberculosis, which her mother had died of, they sent her to a sanatorium with Eve to look after her. The family planned how they would take turns keeping her company through the summer, and in a few months she would be well again.

On the way to the sanatorium, she collapsed in Eve's arms, her temperature soaring. She was in the last stages of radiation sickness, dying from 34 years of breathing radioactive air and touching radioactive substances without properly protecting herself. In a little more than 20 years, it would also kill Irene and Frédéric Joliot.

Marie died on the fourth of July 1934, at the age of 66, and was buried two days later in the grave where Pierre already lay. Even as family, friends, and the many scientists she had so deeply affected by her life and work gathered around the grave, journalists clambered over the cemetery walls. To them, this woman was public property.

To her family, her children and sisters and brother, she was a person of continual inspiration, a source of love and strength since those early days when they had struggled in Poland together.

What was she to the world? In 1922, when the scientists of the Academy of Medicine elected her unanimously to membership, breaking all tradition by allowing a woman into their ranks, they said, "We salute in you a great scientist, a great-hearted woman who has lived only through devotion to work and scientific abnegation, a patriot who, in war and peace, has always done more than her duty. Your presence here brings us the moral benefit of your example and the glory of your name. We thank you. We are proud of your presence among us."

What more could be said of Marie Curie and how can one measure, in this nuclear age, the scale of her contribution to the progress of science and the relief of human suffering?

"At the moment when the fame of the two scientists and benefactors was spreading through the world, grief overtook Marie: her husband, her wonderful companion, was taken from her by death in an instant. But in spite of distress and physical illness, she continued alone the work that had been begun with him and brilliantly developed the science they had created together."

Eve Curie, from her biography, "Madame Curie."

Marie Curie's legacy

Marie Curie left a great deal to the world. Her discovery of radium saved or prolonged the lives of millions of cancer patients. Her work on the structure of the atom helped other scientists develop nuclear power.

She also improved the image of science by pioneering meticulous research methods and founding two research institutes that trained young scientists in her scientific procedures.

As the first woman in Europe to earn a Ph.D. in science, Marie Curie entered a professional world previously barred to women. She was determined that the men who dominated that world would accept her and treat her as an equal.

Most of us know of Curie because she discovered radium. But perhaps her most important scientific discovery came when she learned that radiation came from inside the atom itself. This principle lead to a new field, nuclear physics.

Manufacturers tried to apply what Curie had discovered. Their first inventions were often frivolous — and dangerous to their users, like the radium face powder marketed in the 1920s. But better things followed — radiotherapy that is used to treat cancer, nuclear reactors that generate electrical power, and lasers and radio-isotopes that are used throughout industry for tasks such as checking the thickness of paper during papermaking, measuring the flow of oil through pipelines, and determining how quickly plants use fertilizers.

The most controversial offshoot of Curie's work must be nuclear power. In 1905, as a result of her work, Albert Einstein suggested that there was immense power inside atoms. By the 1930s, scientists knew that splitting the atom would cause a chain reaction that would release untold energy. The military potential was obvious — and frightening. On July 16, 1945, the first atomic bomb was exploded in New Mexico.

Since then, millions of dollars have gone into nuclear research. In 1954, the United States launched a nuclear submarine, the USS Nautilus, and the Soviets began the first civilian nuclear power station.

Nuclear power has great potential as an energy source. But nuclear reactors have two serious drawbacks. First, they produce extremely dangerous wastes that have to be stored for unbelievably long periods of time if they are to lose their radioactivity. Plutonium, for instance, will still be dangerous 24,000 years from now! And no matter how

Inside a modern nuclear fuel power station generating electricity. Marie had worked in much more primitive conditions and had sacrificed her life for scientific research which she believed would benefit mankind.

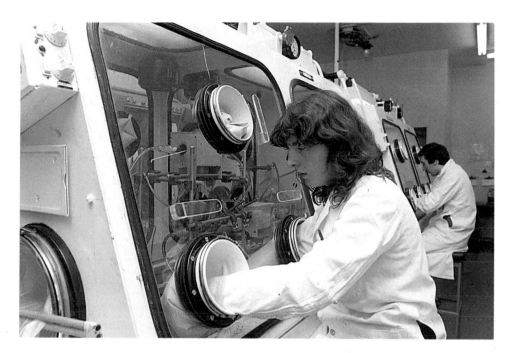

careful we are, some radiation escapes from nuclear reactors. It is relatively small, only about 1.7 percent of the total radiation we are exposed to. But any added radiation is troubling because we are not certain how much radiation we can tolerate. Considering Marie Curie was exposed to radiation every day for nearly twenty-five years with no protection at all, it is amazing she did not succumb to radiation sickness sooner.

Because of their concerns about health, workers in nuclear installations wear protective clothing in all danger areas, and "dosemeters" sound an alarm when too much radiation enters the air.

A second drawback is that nuclear reactors are not foolproof. Something can go wrong. It did in 1987 at the Chernobyl power station in the Soviet Union. After a reactor went out of control, the plant exploded. Fallout scattered over Europe, affecting food and water supplies in many nations. Some Soviet workers lost their lives trying to control the situation.

The power in the atom is there, for good or ill. Marie Curie gave her life to science because she believed in the benefits that could flow to us from scientific research. This was her contribution to humanity. Our challenge is to use wisely the knowledge she unleashed.

No woman before Marie Curie had ever received a science doctorate. She truly pioneered the field of scientific research for women. Many young girls have been inspired by reading about her and today it is common for women to excel in the field of science.

For More Information...

Organizations

The organizations listed below may provide you with more information about radiation and other subjects pertaining to the natural sciences. When you write, be sure to explain what you want to know and remember to include your name, address, and age.

Young Scientists of America
P.O. Box 9066
Phoenix, AZ 85068

Office of Nuclear Technology and Safeguards
Department of State
Washington, D. C. 20520

International Radiation Commission
Science and Engineering Council
Rutherford Appleton Laboratory
Chilton, Didcot OX11 OQX
England

Books

The following books will help you learn more about Marie Curie, other nuclear scientists, and subjects related to nuclear science. Check your local library and bookstore to see if they have them or can order them for you.

About Marie Curie —

A Biography of Marie Sklodowska Curie. Curie, translated by Sheean (Doubleday)
Marie Curie. Bull (David & Charles)
Marie Curie. Keller (Franklin Watts)
Marie Curie. McKnown (Putnam)
Marie Curie: Pioneer Physicist. Greene (Childrens Press)

About Other Nuclear Scientists —

Men and Women Behind The Atom. Riedman (Abelard-Schuman)
The Nuclear Energy Makers. Aaseng (Lerner)
She Lived For Science: Irene Joliot-Curie. McKown (Messner)

About Nuclear Energy and Radiation —

The Great Nuclear Power Debate. Haines (Dodd, Mead)
Inside the Atom. Asimov (Abelard-Schuman)

Nuclear Energy. Coble (Raintree)
Nuclear Energy at the Crossroads. Kiefer (Atheneum)
The Nuclear Energy Controversy. Goode (Franklin Watts)
Nuclear Power: From Physics to Politics. Pringle (Macmillan)
The Nuclear Question. Weiss (Harcourt Brace Jovanovich)
Nuclear Tech Talk. Radlauer and Radlauer (Childrens Press)
Rays and Radiation. Scharff (Putnam)
The Story of Atomic Energy. Fermi (Random)

Magazines

Here are some magazines that feature articles on science, technology, and nature. Look for them in your library, or write to the addresses listed below for information about subscribing. Don't forget to include your name and address.

Current Science
1250 Fairwood Avenue
Columbus, OH 43216

Science Challenge
3500 Western Avenue
Highland Park, IL 60035

3-2-1 Contact
P.O. Box 2933
Boulder, CO 80321

Science World
902 Sylvan Avenue
Englewood Cliffs, NJ 07632

National Geographic World
National Geographic Society
17th and M Streets NW
Washington, D.C. 20036

Glossary

Alpha rays
Particles given off by radioactive substances, discovered by Ernest Rutherford in 1899. They are relatively weak and cannot pierce a sheet of paper. Scientists use them to bombard objects when doing research.

Beta rays
Particles given off by radioactive substances. Stronger than alpha rays, they can penetrate metal and are used to measure the thickness of metals and plastics in industry. Pierre Curie noted differences between beta and alpha rays in 1900.

Cataracts
A disease of the eye. The lens becomes cloudy so that light cannot enter the eye. Marie Curie's cataracts resulted from radiation poisoning.

Curietherapy (also called radiotherapy)
> The treatment of a disease, especially cancer, using radiation — alpha rays, beta rays, or X-rays. Treatments include injecting patients with radioactive gas, exposing the diseased part of the body to rays, or having patients swallow radioactive materials.

Distilling
> Process used in chemistry to purify a liquid by boiling it and condensing the steam. This was one of the many techniques the Curies used to collect radium.

Element
> A basic substance that scientists cannot separate into a simpler substance by chemical means. Of the 105 elements, 93 are natural and 12 are manmade. Oxygen, helium, carbon, nitrogen, and hydrogen are some of the simpler elements.

Emanation
> A gas produced by the radioactive decay of a substance. The Curies worked in air filled with emanations from radioactive substances. It contributed to the radioactive poisoning that eventually killed Marie Curie.

Filtering
> A process used in chemistry to purify a liquid by letting it soak through a porous substance that catches suspended particles. Often, the liquid is useful only in its purified form.

Gamma rays
> Strongest of all radiation, having the same nature as light rays and X-rays. Gamma rays can penetrate the body. When diagnosing a medical problem, physicians can use it to follow the course of radioactive materials inside the patient. Paul-Ulrich Villard discovered gamma rays in 1900.

Nuclear power
> Power that depends upon radioactivity for its source. In power plants, the reaction of radioactive substances is controlled so as to cause heat, which is then used to produce electricity. Nuclear power is also used in submarines. While nuclear power is efficient and long-lasting, it can also be very dangerous. No one has figured out a safe way to store the radioactive waste produced in these plants.

Particle
> Matter so small that it cannot be measured for size but that moves and has magnetic power. Atoms are particles, and the even smaller protons and neutrons within atoms are called particles (or subatomaic particles). Scientists involved in particle theory continue to find tinier and tinier particles within atoms.

Radiation sickness

Disease produced by overexposure to alpha, beta, gamma, or X-rays. Symptoms include vomiting, diarrhea, bleeding, hair loss, cancer, and sterility. At first, people who worked with radioactive material didn't know the damage it could do and died of radiation poisoning.

Radioactivity

Giving off radiation from a substance either because the nuclei of atoms are not stable or because a nuclear reaction has occurred. The radiation includes alpha particles, electrons, nucleons (which are protons or neutrons), and gamma rays. Most things, including plants and animals, have a small amount of radioactivity, which is usually Carbon 14. It is a helpful form of radioactivity for archeologists. The nuclei of the carbon starts to decay as soon as plants, animals, and humans die, so when scientists want to know the age of an archeological find, they can measure the amount of radioactivity present and figure out when the plant or animal began to decay. In 1934, Irene and Frédéric Joliet-Curie produced **artificial radioactivity** in non-radioactive substances by exposing them to radioactive substances.

X-rays

Radiation caused by bombarding heavy atoms with electrons. X-rays are strong enough to pass through much of the body. In small doses, they are weak enough not to cause the body harm. By placing a part of the body between X-rays and photographic film, physicians can take "pictures" of the bones and organs and can then determine what might be wrong with a patient.

Chronology

1867   Marya Sklodowska, called Manya by her family, is born in Warsaw, Poland, the youngest of five children.

1876   Manya's beloved sister, Sophia, dies of typhus fever.

1878   Manya's mother dies of tuberculosis.

1883   Manya graduates from secondary school with a gold medal for scholarship and then spends a year resting in the country.

1884   Manya returns to Warsaw and joins the Floating University.

1885   Manya and her sister Bronya begin work as governesses to earn money to go to school in Paris. Bronya goes first.

1890   Manya goes to Paris to begin studying at the Sorbonne, the University of Paris, where she changes her name to Marie, the French version of Marya.

1892	Marie moves out of Bronya's house to be near the university.
1893	Marie passes physics at the head of her class.
1894	Marie passes her second exams for a degree in mathematics. She meets Pierre Curie.
1895	**July 26** — Pierre and Marie marry. **November 8** — Wilhelm Röntgen discovers X-rays.
1896	**February 28** — Henri Becquerel discovers radioactivity.
1897	**September** — Irene Curie is born. Marie begins researching radioactivity.
1898	**April 12** — Marie presents her first paper to Academie des Sciences, the prestigious scientific organization in France. **June 6** — Marie isolates polonium.
1899	Marie begins process of isolating radium from pitchblende.
1902	She completes process of isolating radium.
1903	Marie presents her doctoral thesis, becoming the first woman in Europe to be awarded a doctorate. Along with Henri Becquerel, Marie and Pierre are awarded the Nobel Prize for Physics for their work on radioactivity.
1904	**December** — Eve Curie is born.
1906	**April 19** — Pierre Curie is killed by a horse-drawn cart. **November 15** — Marie takes over Pierre's classes and is the first woman to teach at the Sorbonne.
1911	Marie wins the Nobel Prize for Chemistry.
1912	Marie is named Director of the Radium Institute in Paris.
1914	**July 31** — The Radium Institute is completed. **August 4** — World War I begins.
1914-18	Marie organizes mobile X-ray units for use at the battle front. She trains 150 operators during World War I.
1921	Marie tours the United States to raise funds for research. President

Harding presents one gram of radium to Marie as a gift from the people of the United States of America.

1922   Marie is made a member of the League of Nations' International Committee on Intellectual Cooperation.

1926   Irene Curie marries Frédéric Joliot.

1929   Marie goes to the United States and returns to France with another gram of radium presented by President Hoover.

1934   The Joliot-Curies discover radioactivity can be made artificially.
July 5 — Marie Curie dies.

1935   Irene and Frédéric Joliot-Curie receive the Nobel Prize for Physics.

1937   Eve Curie publishes *Madame Curie*, the biography of her mother.

1944   The first atomic bomb explodes at Alamogordo, New Mexico.

Index